D0385689

Friendship

Friendship

Running Press
Philadelphia, Pennsylvania

A Running Press Miniature Edition

Copyright © 1989 by Running Press.
Printed in Hong Kong
All rights reserved under the Pan-American and
International Copyright Conventions.

*This book may not be reproduced in whole or in part in
any form or by any means, electronic or mechanical,
including photocopying, recording, or by any information
storage and retrieval system now known or hereafter
invented, without written permission from the publisher.*

Canadian representatives: General Publishing Co., Ltd.,
30 Lesmill Road, Don Mills, Ontario M3B 2T6.

International representatives: Worldwide Media Services.
Inc., 115 East Twenty-third Street, New York, NY 10010

9   8
Digit on the right indicates the number of this printing.
Library of Congress Catalog Card Number: 88-43563
ISBN 0-89471-716-2

This book may be ordered by mail from the publisher.
Please add $1.00 for postage and handling.
But try your bookstore first!
Running Press Book Publishers
125 South Twenty-second Street
Philadelphia, Pennsylvania 19103

INTRODUCTION

Who knows us better than our friends? Friends share with us, count on us, and comfort us. They improve the quality of our lives, raise our spiritual standard of living, and are not too polite to tell us when we have a bit of thread dangling from one sleeve.

When we're with them, we don't have to dress up, or put out the guest towels, or even finish our sentences. Friends know us better than that.

Through the quotations in this book, some of the world's greatest writers, artists, thinkers, and leaders—

from Jane Austin to Will Rogers, and from Margaret Mead to Mao Tse-tung—express their views on friendship. They embrace its sweetness, respect its scarcity, and occasionally pucker at its tang.

Each friendship is unique, but the need for friends and the pleasures of friendship are universal.

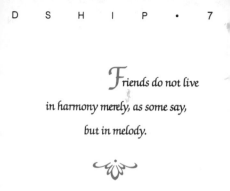

$\mathcal{F}$riends do not live

in harmony merely, as some say,

but in melody.

HENRY DAVID THOREAU (1817–1862)
American writer

Some of

my best friends are children.

In fact, all of my best friends are children.

J.D. SALINGER, b. 1919
American writer

Grief can take care of itself, but to get the full value of a joy you must have somebody to divide it with.

MARK TWAIN (1835–1910)
American writer

There are three types of friends: those like food, without which you can't live; those like medicine, which you need occasionally; and those like an illness, which you never want.

SOLOMON IBN GABIROL (1021–1058)
Hebrew poet, aphorist

If you have

one true friend you have

more than your share.

THOMAS FULLER (1654–1734)
English physician, writer

A friend

is one who dislikes

the same people you dislike.

ANONYMOUS

It is said

that love is blind. Friendship,

on the other hand, is clairvoyant.

PHILIPPE SOUPAULT, b. 1897
French writer

Platonic

love is love from the neck up.

THYRA SAMTER WINSLOW (1903–1961)
American drama and literary critic

"*Yes'm, old friends is always best, 'less you can catch a new one that's fit to make an old one out of.*"

SARAH ORNE JEWETT (1849–1909)
American writer

I want everyone else
I meet in the whole world to like me,
except the people I've already met, handled,
found inconsequential, and forgot about.

JOSEPH HELLER, b. 1923
American writer

*S*ooner or later
you've heard about all
your best friends have to say.
Then comes the tolerance of real love.

NED ROREM, b. 1923
American composer

Having
someone wonder where you are
when you don't come home at night
is a very old human need.

MARGARET MEAD (1901–1978)
American anthropologist

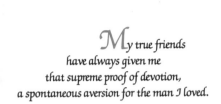

My true friends
have always given me
that supreme proof of devotion,
a spontaneous aversion for the man I loved.

COLETTE (1873–1954)
French writer

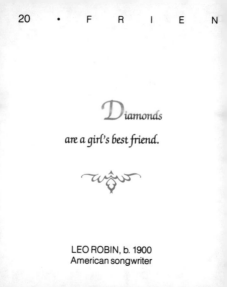

Diamonds

are a girl's best friend.

LEO ROBIN, b. 1900
American songwriter

Here at the frontier, there are falling leaves.
Although my neighbors are all barbarians,
And you, you are a thousand miles away,
There are always two cups on my table.

ANONYMOUS
(T'ang Dynasty, A.D. 618–906)

The bird a nest,

the spider a web, man friendship.

WILLIAM BLAKE (1757–1827)
English poet, painter

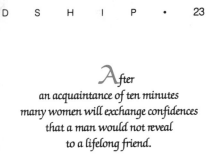

After
an acquaintance of ten minutes
many women will exchange confidences
that a man would not reveal
to a lifelong friend.

PAGE SMITH, b. 1917
American historian

If we all told

what we know of one another there

would not be four friends in the world.

BLAISE PASCAL (1623–1662)
French philosopher

How

I like to be liked,

and what I do to be liked!

CHARLES LAMB (1775–1834)
English writer

We

tiptoed around each other

like heartbreaking new friends.

JACK KEROUAC (1922–1969)
American writer

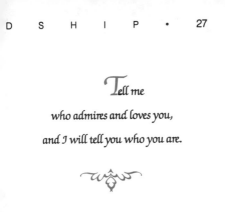

Tell me

who admires and loves you,

and I will tell you who you are.

CHARLES AUGUSTIN SAINTE-BEUVE
(1804–1869)
French critic

I want
someone to laugh with me,
someone to be grave with me,
someone to please me and help my
discrimination with his or her own
remark, and at times, no doubt, to admire
my acuteness and penetration.

ROBERT BURNS (1759–1796)
Scottish poet

I do not want
people to be very agreeable, as it saves me
the trouble of liking them a great deal.

JANE AUSTEN (1775–1817)
English writer

My friends,

there are no friends.

COCO CHANEL (1883–1971)
French fashion designer

Friendship

is far more tragic than love.

It lasts longer.

OSCAR WILDE (1854–1900)
English writer

$\mathcal{H}$e who is

the friend of all humanity

is not my friend.

MOLIÈRE (1622–1673)
French playwright

*O*h dear!

how unfortunate I am

not to have anyone to weep with!

MADAME DE SÉVIGNÉ (1626–1696)
French writer

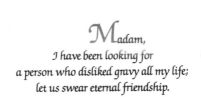

Madam,
I have been looking for
a person who disliked gravy all my life;
let us swear eternal friendship.

SYDNEY SMITH (1771–1845)
English clergyman

$\mathcal{M}$y darling,

be a wife, be a friend, write good letters,

do not mope, do not torment me.

ANTON CHEKOV (1860–1904)
Russian writer

I want

a sofa, as I want a friend,

upon which I can repose familiarly.

WILLIAM MAKEPEACE THACKERAY
(1811–1863)
English writer

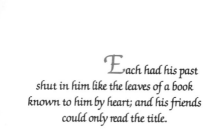

*Each had his past
shut in him like the leaves of a book
known to him by heart; and his friends
could only read the title.*

VIRGINIA WOOLF (1882–1941)
English writer

Most people

enjoy the inferiority

of their friends.

LORD CHESTERFIELD (1694–1773)

*W*hen people
have light in themselves,
it will shine out from them.
Then we get to know each other
as we walk together in the darkness,
without needing to pass our hands
over each other's faces, or to intrude
into each other's hearts.

ALBERT SCHWEITZER (1875–1965)
German scholar, humanitarian

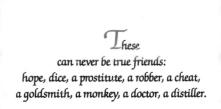

These
can never be true friends:
hope, dice, a prostitute, a robber, a cheat,
a goldsmith, a monkey, a doctor, a distiller.

HINDU PROVERB

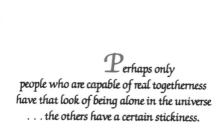

*Perhaps only
people who are capable of real togetherness
have that look of being alone in the universe
. . . the others have a certain stickiness.*

D.H. LAWRENCE (1885–1930)
English writer

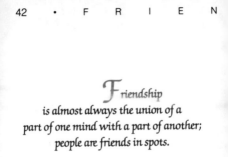

Friendship
is almost always the union of a
part of one mind with a part of another;
people are friends in spots.

GEORGE SANTAYANA (1863–1952)
American writer

I step over
to his table and give him a medium hello,
and he looks up and gives me a medium
hello right back, for, to tell you the truth,
Maury and I are never bosom friends.

DAMON RUNYON (1880–1946)
American writer

Treat your friends as you do your pictures, and place them in their best light.

JENNIE JEROME CHURCHILL (1854–1921)
English writer (mother of Winston Churchill)

$\mathcal{A}$nimals

are such agreeable friends—they

ask no questions, they pass no criticisms.

GEORGE ELIOT (1819–1880)
English writer

When a person that one loves is in the world and alive and well... then to miss them is only a new flavor, a salt sharpness in experience.

WINIFRED HOLTBY (1898–1935)
English writer

One passes
through the world knowing few,
if any, of the important things about
even the people with whom one has
been . . . in the closest intimacy.

ANTHONY POWELL, b. 1905
English writer

One friend

in a lifetime is much; two are many;

three are hardly possible.

HENRY ADAMS (1838–1918)
American writer

A friend knows

how to allow for mere quantity in

your talk, and only replies to the quality…

WILLIAM DEAN HOWELLS (1837–1920)
American writer

To find

a friend one must close one eye:

to keep him, two.

NORMAN DOUGLAS (1868–1952)
English novelist, scientist

Every murderer is probably somebody's old friend.

AGATHA CHRISTIE (1890–1976)
English writer

Think

twice before you speak

to a friend in need.

AMBROSE BIERCE (1842–1914)
American writer

Friendship

is like money, easier made

than kept.

SAMUEL BUTLER (1835–1902)
English novelist, essayist

*Unfortunately,
in a long life one gets barnacled over
with the mere shells of friendship
and it is difficult without hurting oneself
to scrape them off.*

BERNARD BERENSON (1865–1959)
Polish/American art critic

*I*nstead

of loving your enemies,

treat your friends a little better.

EDGAR WATSON HOWE (1853–1937)
American writer

Constant

use had not worn ragged

the fabric of their friendship.

DOROTHY PARKER (1893–1967)
American writer

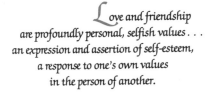

Love and friendship
are profoundly personal, selfish values . . .
an expression and assertion of self-esteem,
a response to one's own values
in the person of another.

AYN RAND, (1905–1982)
Russian/American writer

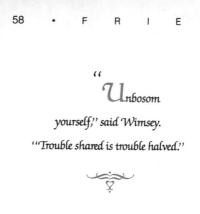

"
Unbosom

yourself," said *Wimsey.*

"Trouble shared is trouble halved."

DOROTHY SAYERS (1893–1957)
English writer

All the world

is queer save thee and me.

And even thou art a little queer.

ROBERT OWEN (1771–1858)
Welsh/American social reformer

W_{hat}

I cannot love, I overlook.

Is that real friendship?

ANAÏS NIN (1903–1977)
French/American writer

$\mathcal{H}$istories

are more full of examples

of the fidelity of dogs than of friends.

ALEXANDER POPE (1688–1744)
English poet

Only choose

in marriage a woman whom you

would choose as a friend if she were a man.

JOSEPH JOUBERT (1754–1824)
French philosopher

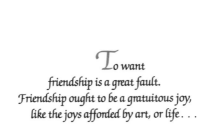

$\mathcal{T}$o want
friendship is a great fault.
Friendship ought to be a gratuitous joy,
like the joys afforded by art, or life . . .

SIMONE WEIL (1909–1943)
French philosopher

$\mathcal{M}$oney

can't buy friends,

but you can get a better class of enemy.

~~~

SPIKE MILLIGAN, b. 1918
English comedian, writer

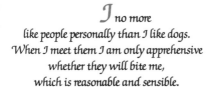

I no more
like people personally than *I* like dogs.
When *I* meet them *I* am only apprehensive
whether they will bite me,
which is reasonable and sensible.

STANLEY SPENCER (1891–1959)
English artist

We need

two kinds of acquaintances, one to

complain to, while we boast to the others.

LOGAN PEARSALL SMITH (1865–1946)
American/English writer

$\mathcal{I}$t is in
the thirties that we want friends.
In the forties we know they won't save us
any more than love did.

F. SCOTT FITZGERALD (1896–1940)
American writer

. . . *O*urs,

that tea bag of a word

which steeps in the conditional.

ELIZABETH HARDWICK, b. 1916
American writer, educator

Choose

an author as you

choose a friend.

WENTWORTH DILLON, Earl of Roscommon
(1633–1685)
English nobleman

Because
I got you to look after me,
and you got me to look after you . . .
We got each other, that's what,
that gives a hoot in hell about us . . .

JOHN STEINBECK (1902–1968)
American writer

$\mathcal{F}$riends

to borrow my books

and set wet glasses on them.

EDWIN ARLINGTON ROBINSON (1869–1935)
American poet

If you want

a person's faults, go to those who love him.

They will not tell you, but they know.

ROBERT LOUIS STEVENSON (1850–1894)
Scottish writer

And the song,

from beginning to end,

I found in the heart of a friend.

HENRY WADSWORTH LONGFELLOW
(1807–1882)
American poet

*There was
nothing remote or mysterious here—
only something private. The only secret
was the ancient communication
between two people.*

EUDORA WELTY, b. 1909
American writer

If I had to choose between betraying my country and betraying my friend, I hope I should have the guts to betray my country.

E.M. FORSTER (1879–1970)
English writer

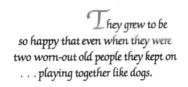

*They grew to be
so happy that even when they were
two worn-out old people they kept on
. . . playing together like dogs.*

GABRIEL GARCIA MARQUEZ, b. 1928
Colombian writer

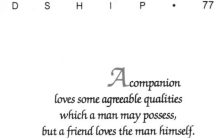

A companion
loves some agreeable qualities
which a man may possess,
but a friend loves the man himself.

JAMES BOSWELL (1740–1795)
Scottish biographer, lawyer

The

differences between friends

cannot but reinforce their friendship.

MAO TSE-TUNG (1893–1976)
Chinese leader

A woman
wants her friends to be perfect.
She sets a pattern . . . lays a friend out
on this pattern and worries and prods
at any little qualities which do not
coincide with her own image.

BETTY MACDONALD (1908–1958)
American writer

The

richer your friends,

the more they will cost you.

ELISABETH MARBURY (1856–1933)
American theatrical agent

*B*eing with you

is like walking on a very clear morning—

definitely the sensation of belonging there.

E.B. WHITE (1899–1985)
American writer

Friendship
is unnecessary, like philosophy, like art . . .
It has no survival value; rather it is one of
those things that give value to survival.

C.S. LEWIS (1898–1963)
English writer

I no doubt

deserved my enemies, but I don't believe

I deserved my friends.

WALT WHITMAN (1819–1892)
American poet

$\mathcal{F}$riends

are a second existence.

BALTASAR GRACIAN (1601–1658)
Spanish satirist, writer

The only thing

to do is to hug one's friends tight

and do one's job.

EDITH WHARTON (1862–1937)
American writer

If two people
who love each other let a single instant
wedge itself between them, it grows—
it becomes a month, a year, a century;
it becomes too late.

JEAN GIRAUDOUX (1882–1944)
French playwright

It is good

to have some friends

both in Heaven and in Hell.

GEORGE HERBERT (1593–1633)
English writer

$\mathcal{F}$riendship

is a very taxing and

arduous form of leisure activity.

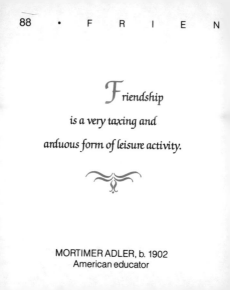

MORTIMER ADLER, b. 1902
American educator

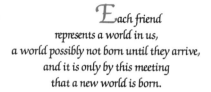

*Each friend
represents a world in us,
a world possibly not born until they arrive,
and it is only by this meeting
that a new world is born.*

ANAÏS NIN (1903–1977)
French/American writer

*W*hat is

important to a relationship is a harmony

of emotional roles and not too great a

disparity in the general level of intelligence.

MIRRA KOMAROVSKY, b. 1906
Russian/American educator

*F*riendship

or love—one must choose.

One cannot serve two masters.

RENÉ CREVEL (1900–1935)
French writer

Wherever

you are it is your own friends

who make your world.

WILLIAM JAMES (1842–1910)
American psychologist and philosopher

$\mathcal{L}$ouis,

I think this is the

beginning of a beautiful friendship.

RICK BLAINE
Saloon owner (in the film *Casablanca*)

Running Press Miniature Editions™

Aesop's Fables
As a Man Thinketh
A Child's Garden of Verses
Emily Dickinson: Selected Poems
Friendship: A Bouquet of Quotes
The Literary Cat
Love: Quotations from the Heart
Quotable Women
Sherlock Holmes: Two Complete Adventures
Sonnets from the Portuguese
The Velveteen Rabbit

This book has been bound using handcraft methods, and Smythe-sewn to ensure durability.

The dust jacket was designed by Toby Schmidt. The interior design and calligraphic design elements were created by Judith Barbour Osborne. The text was typeset in Zapf Chancery Medium and Triumvirate Book by Commcor Communications Corporation, Philadelphia, Pennsylvania.